C0-AAY-407

BOWLING

CONSULTANTS

Charles Hall
Executive Secretary,
American Junior Bowling Congress

June Zamis
Expert Bowler

Robby Robinson
Professional Bowler and Teacher

Ned Day
Former World's Individual
Match Game Champion

Milton Raymer
Former Executive Secretary,
American Junior Bowling Congress

ATHLETIC INSTITUTE SERIES

STERLING PUBLISHING CO., INC.   **NEW YORK**

Foreword

"Bowling" is one of a comprehensive series of sports instruction aids made available on a non-profit basis by The Athletic Institute. The photographic material in this book has been reproduced in total from The Athletic Institute's sound, color slidefilm, "Beginning Bowling." This book and the slidefilm are parts of a program designed to bring the many benefits of athletics, physical education and recreation to everyone.

The Athletic Institute is a non-profit organization devoted to the advancement of athletics, recreation and physical education. It functions on the premise that athletics and recreation brings benefits of inestimable value to the individual and to the community.

The nature and scope of the many Athletic Institute programs are determined by an advisory committee of selected persons noted for their outstanding knowledge, experience and ability in the fields of athletics, physical education and recreation.

It is their hope, and the hope of The Athletic Institute, that through the use of this book, the reader will become a better bowler, skilled in the fundamentals of this fine, exciting game. In addition to instructional material on bowling itself, there are included sections on the history of the sport, and on the etiquette of the sport. The good bowler is the bowler who not only scores well, but who also knows the sport thoroughly, and lives by its rules, written and unwritten.

Knowledge, and the practice necessary to mold knowledge into playing ability, are the keys to real bowling enjoyment.

THE SPIN AND SCORING PARTS OF
THIS PUBLICATION PLUS OTHER MATERIAL
WERE TAKEN FROM THE BOOK
"BOWLING (TIPS AND LESSONS)
BY ROBBY ROBINSON"

Fourth Printing, 1966

Copyright © 1962 by The Athletic Institute
Published by Sterling Publishing Co., Inc.
419 Fourth Avenue, New York 16, N.Y.
Manufactured in the United States of America
All rights reserved
Library of Congress Catalog Card No.: 62-21019

CONTENTS

HISTORY

Good exercise in a heathful atmosphere . . . good competition and good fun with good friends . . . that's bowling, America's most popular indoor sport with almost 30 million men, women, and children enjoying it regularly. Although bowling is a popular modern game, it is also one of the world's oldest sports.

As far back as five thousand B.C., seven thousand years ago, the children of Egypt played a game similar to our twentieth-century bowling.

But the American game comes more directly from Germany, where the game started to develop around the start of the Christian era. At that time, no German man would appear in public without a small wooden club called his kegel.

Although their kegels often came in handy as weapons of self-defense, primarily they were used for recreation. People who played with kegels in those days were called "kegelers" and today, more than one thousand years later, bowlers are often called "keglers."

The kegel was also a part of the religious ordeals of the early Germans. In the cloisters of the church, they were often required to set up their kegel, and ...

... throw a round stone at it. In the trial the kegel was called heide, or heathen. If the man could knock the heide down, he proved to the priest's satisfaction that he had been living an honorable life.

Soon the priests recognized the recreational value of this religious kegeling and started to amuse themselves with it. All the participants of the game would set their kegels down together and each would bowl in turn to see how many he could knock down with a single ball.

Soon the religious recreation spread outside the cloisters and through the following centuries, kegeling became a popular sport in Germany.

In the fifteenth century, Martin Luther was an enthusiastic kegeler and it was he who, after long experiment, standardized the number of pins at nine and drew up the basic rules for the game.

As the game spread, people started to build wooden lanes and cover them against the rain. Balls improved and the pins were given a better shape. Kegeling was established as an important part of European recreation.

The Dutch were great bowlers and when they came to this country as settlers in New Amsterdam, New York, they brought the game with them and set up America's first bowling lanes in 1623.

The arrangement of pins they used was the same as they had used in Europe since the days of Martin Luther—nine pins in three straight rows, with one corner pointing toward the bowler. But these early Americans were pioneering new things. European styles were being replaced.

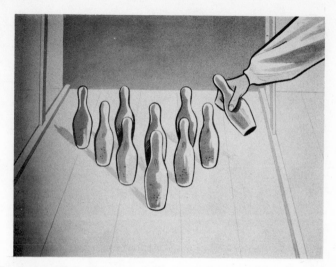

So they applied new science to bowling, added another pin and developed a triangular arrangement. Soon, ten pins, set in a triangle, became the standard for bowling everywhere in America.

Today the same ten-pin set-up is still standard and ever since that day, bowling has grown in popularity until now . . .

. . . bowling has grown up with America. It has outgrown the pioneer days and became a sport with its own fine standing in every community from the metropolitan centers to the smallest hamlets.

Bowling is a favorite sport of thirty million Americans of all ages . . . both sexes, a game for everyone from eight to eighty . . .

a game in which thousands of people from factories and offices find fun and physical exercise with their co-workers . . .

for throughout the country, the bowling lanes have become centers of community recreation, developing a community spirit of unity and friend-liness.

The modern bowling lane is a masterpiece of scientific design and construction. Built of maple and pine, the surface is leveled so that no section is more than forty-thousandths of an inch lower or higher than any other section. Along each side of the lane is a channel. At one side is the track along which the ball is sent back to the bowler, called the ball return.

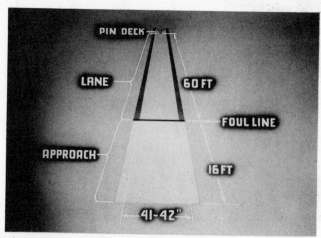

The lane consists of a sixteen-foot approach ending at the foul line. Then, a sixty-foot lane from the foul line to the first pin. The area where the pins are set is called the pin deck. The lane is forty-one to forty-two inches wide.

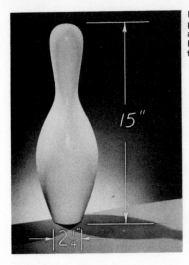

Made of wood or plastic, the standard pin is fifteen inches high and two-and-a-quarter inches in diameter at the base. It weighs approximately three to three-and-a-half pounds.

Ten pins are set in a standard triangular arrangement, with twelve inches between all pins, center to center.

The first pin, called the head pin, is number one. The rest are numbered consecutively in their rows from left to right. Pins in the second row, left to right, are 2 and 3. Third row, left to right, are 4, 5, and 6. Fourth row, left to right, are 7, 8, 9, and 10.

As a bowler delivers the ball down the lane, he slides with one foot while the other stays back for balance. Therefore, bowlers must have special shoes —one shoe to make sliding easy, and the other to hold traction on the approach.

To provide traction, the sole of one shoe is made of composition rubber with a leather tip. The other is made of leather or a harder composition for sliding. If you bowl right-handed, you slide on your left foot, so your left shoe should have the sliding leather sole. If you bowl left-handed, the sole of your right shoe should be leather. While shoes are the only special equipment a beginning bowler needs...

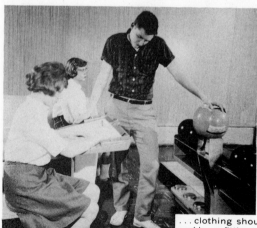

...clothing should be comfortable and loose fitting to allow free and easy movement of arms and legs.

The regulation bowling ball varies in weight between ten and sixteen pounds and must not exceed twenty-seven inches in circumference. There is also a ball weighing nine pounds for childrens' use.

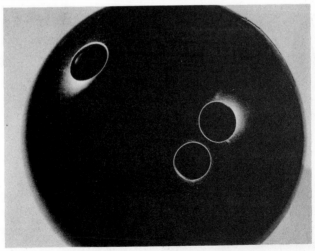

Almost all bowlers today use the three-finger ball . . . a ball drilled with three holes to be gripped with the thumb and two fingers.

When you bowl, you should use a ball that fits <u>your</u> hand to bowl your best game.

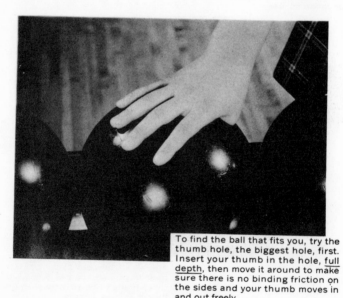

To find the ball that fits you, try the thumb hole, the biggest hole, first. Insert your thumb in the hole, <u>full depth</u>, then move it around to make sure there is no binding friction on the sides and your thumb moves in and out freely.

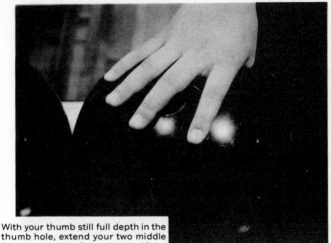

With your thumb still full depth in the thumb hole, extend your two middle fingers over the finger holes. If the ball is the right fit, the second joints of your fingers will extend at least a quarter of an inch over the inside edge of the holes.

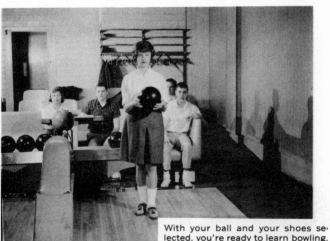

With your ball and your shoes selected, you're ready to learn bowling. You're going to enjoy learning and you'll enjoy playing for many years, but you'll enjoy it more if you and your partners observe the simple rules of safety and etiquette.

17

Here's a bowler who forgot a safety rule by picking his ball from the ball return the wrong way and he's still doing it wrong. A ball coming up the return would hurt his fingers again. There's a right and safe way to pick up your ball.

Simply grasp it with both hands on the outside—not inside, where a returning ball might hit them. When picking up your ball, always stay alert for other balls coming through the ball return.

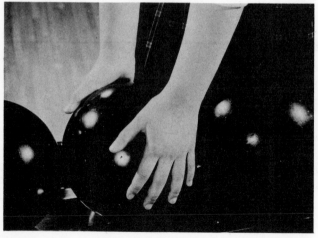

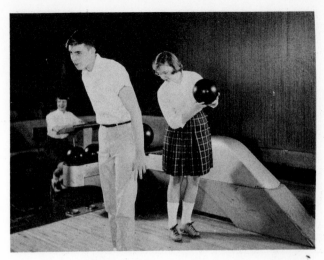

And never try to practice swings while awaiting your turn to bowl.

Someone walking behind you might get hurt. There's only one safe time to swing a bowling ball, and that's when you're actually bowling.

The bowler who forgets his turn and isn't ready, delays the game and spoils the fun for the others. Keep track of the game and be ready for your turn.

Many bowlers have their own personal ball which is usually identified by their initials. Remember, it is their personal property and don't use it unless they invite you to.

Learn to identify your own ball by its number or some other marking. Don't delay the game searching among all the balls on the return and trying to remember which is yours.

Bowling requires intensive concentration. From the time a bowler takes his starting position until he completes his delivery, any movement in a lane on either side can break his concentration and ruin his delivery.

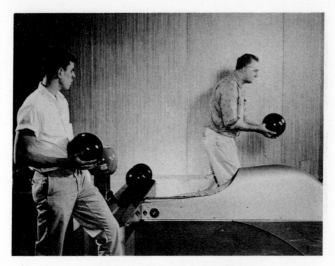

If a bowler in the lane next to you has taken his stance and is ready to bowl, stay back off the approach until he has taken the first step of his delivery. Then...

...quickly step up to the rack, get your ball, and take your turn.

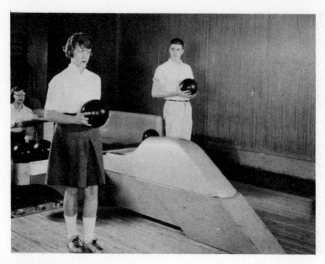

If you and the bowler next to you should both be ready to bowl at the same time, the rule of etiquette is very simple . . .

. . . always give way to the bowler on your right. By the same token, the bowler on your left should let you go first. Before you bowl . . .

. . . be sure the pin-setting machine "sweeper" has returned to the "up" position and is fully clear of the pins. Otherwise, your ball may strike the

sweeper with considerable force and cause not only damage to the mechanism, but a delay in your game.

After you have bowled, come back to the starting point on your approach, or you may collide with a bowler on the next lane. Dont wander about the approach or remain at the foul line longer than is necessary to see how many pins you have knocked down.

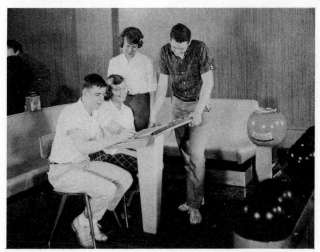

Bowling is good fun and good exercise from the very first game, whether your score is good or bad. As your score improves, your fun will improve too. If you learn the fundamentals of approach and delivery now, your score will improve faster and you will easily develop a skill that will last throughout your lifetime.

2

DELIVERY

Whether you're an expert bowler or a
beginner at the sport, there's fun,
excitement and good exercise in
bowling.

But when you're a good bowler...
when the first ball takes all the pins
in one clean sweep...

...there's the added thrill of achieve-
ment and satisfaction of skill.

While some beginning bowlers seem to have a natural ability for the game, anyone can <u>become</u> a good bowler. It's only a matter of knowing the fundamentals of skill and then practicing them until they feel easy and natural.

For reasons of simplicity, the instruction throughout this series is designed for right-handed bowlers. The technique for left-handed bowlers is exactly the same . . .

. . . except that it is reversed. The left foot forward for the right-handed bowler becomes the right foot forward for the left-handed bowler, a right-hand wrist action becomes a left-hand wrist action and so on.

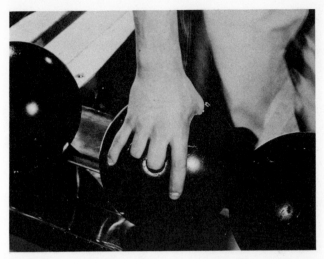

The first fundamental is grip. Select a ball that fits your hand. Then set your thumb in the thumb hole— middle fingers in the finger holes— and let the index and little fingers rest flat against the ball in whatever position is most natural and comfortable for you.

The delivery in bowling is not a throw or a pitch. Your body sets up forward momentum for the ball as you approach the foul line. Then your arm carries the momentum through to the ball as it swings forward naturally. You neither throw nor push. You simply set the ball in motion.

Before learning the complete delivery,
let's get the feeling of the ball and
the basic action of the delivery as the
ball leaves your hand.

There is the critical movement in your delivery . . . the forward swing where your arm picks up the momentum from your body and carries it through to the ball. To get the feel of the swing, let's try just this much of it, as a preliminary exercise.

Stand at the foul line with your <u>left foot</u> slightly forward and the ball hanging at the full extent of your arm. Don't bend your elbow or try to hold the ball up. Just let it hang with your arm and shoulder relaxed. Feel the weight of the ball in your shoulder.

Your arm should be turned so that your thumb points in the direction you want the ball to travel.

Now bend your knees slightly and lean your body forward so that the ball is well below your knee. Let the ball hang. Don't try to hold it up.

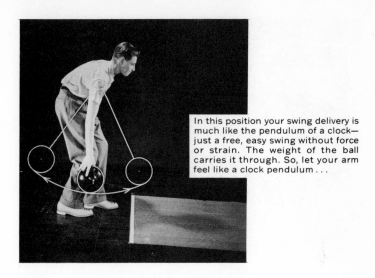

In this position your swing delivery is much like the pendulum of a clock— just a free, easy swing without force or strain. The weight of the ball carries it through. So, let your arm feel like a clock pendulum . . .

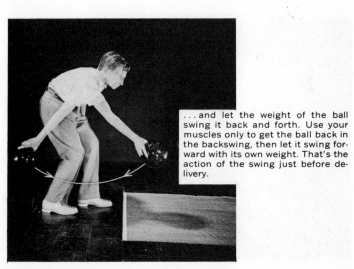

. . . and let the weight of the ball swing it back and forth. Use your muscles only to get the ball back in the backswing, then let it swing forward with its own weight. That's the action of the swing just before delivery.

In releasing the ball in the delivery, your thumb, which has been leading the swing, slips out of the hole first. Then, the ball simply rolls off your finger tips as your hand and arm swing on through the upward arc.

The ball leaves your hand just ahead of your left foot which is at the foul line. Deliver the ball over the foul line. When you release the ball your hand should be started on its upward arc. The weight of the ball actually pulls it from your hand.

Don't hang on to the ball too long.
If you release it after your arm is too
high on the upward arc, you will spoil
your delivery and harm the surface
of the lane.

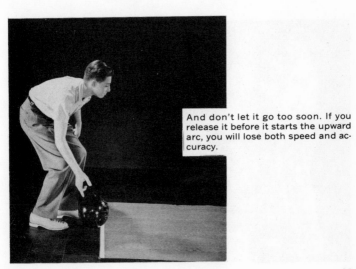

And don't let it go too soon. If you
release it before it starts the upward
arc, you will lose both speed and accuracy.

There is the swing. Practice this swing delivery until the ball seems to leave your hand naturally and your hand swings on upward in a free follow through. Don't try to force the ball—don't push it or throw it. Just let it swing forward like a pendulum and let go so that it rolls away smoothly.

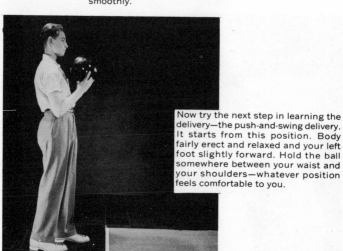

Now try the next step in learning the delivery—the push-and-swing delivery. It starts from this position. Body fairly erect and relaxed and your left foot slightly forward. Hold the ball somewhere between your waist and your shoulders—whatever position feels comfortable to you.

Your right hand has the correct grip
and your left supports the ball.

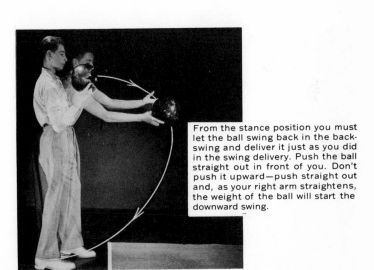

From the stance position you must
let the ball swing back in the back-
swing and deliver it just as you did
in the swing delivery. Push the ball
straight out in front of you. Don't
push it upward—push straight out
and, as your right arm straightens,
the weight of the ball will start the
downward swing.

As your arm straightens out into the pendulum position, start bending your knees to get into the slightly crouched position of the swing delivery.

From there, the delivery is the same as the swing delivery you practiced earlier. Let the ball swing back at the end of your arm . . . then forward. Practice this push-and-swing delivery until the ball moves from your body, outward, down and back in smooth rhythm. It's the length of this back-swing—not the force you put into it—that determines the speed of your ball. Take it easy and let the weight of the ball do most of the work.

If you have mastered the push-and-swing delivery, you're ready for the full approach delivery. There is the complete movement for the four-step delivery—footwork, swing and follow-through timed in a rhythmic movement. Timing and rhythm are important in bowling and the basic factor of timing is footwork. Everything is coordinated with the movement of your feet on the approach. One of the best ways to learn the proper footwork is by first practicing it without the ball ...

... selecting a starting position that will let you take your four steps forward and still finish behind the foul line. A rule of thumb for selecting your starting position is to use the 12-foot marker as a guide, and take four and a half normal walking steps forward.

Remember, the foul line is only there to remind you to stay behind it as you finish your delivery. There is no exact spot at which you should finish so don't feel that you have to come right up to the foul line every time.

Most experienced bowlers finish their deliveries anywhere from six to two inches behind the foul line. Allow yourself enough room for a comfortable delivery and always remember . . . if your four steps don't take you up close to the foul line, never take an extra step to get there. This will simply throw your timing off and result in a poorly rolled ball. Instead, adjust your approach by beginning further forward of the 12-foot marker.

To begin the delivery . . .

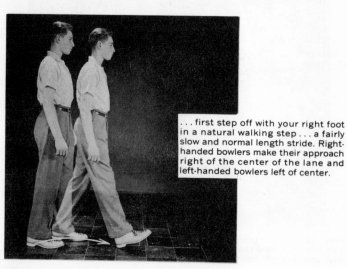

. . . first step off with your right foot in a natural walking step . . . a fairly slow and normal length stride. Right-handed bowlers make their approach right of the center of the lane and left-handed bowlers left of center.

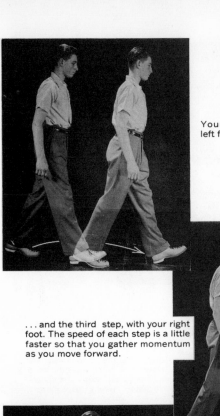

Your second step is taken with the left foot . . .

. . . and the third step, with your right foot. The speed of each step is a little faster so that you gather momentum as you move forward.

The fourth step, with your left foot, is more of a slide than a step . . . with the left foot leaving the floor only slightly . . .

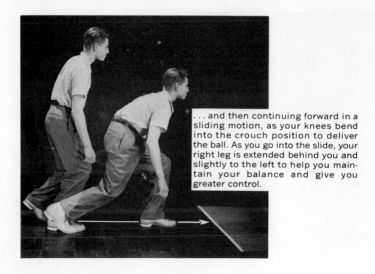

. . . and then continuing forward in a sliding motion, as your knees bend into the crouch position to deliver the ball. As you go into the slide, your right leg is extended behind you and slightly to the left to help you maintain your balance and give you greater control.

There is the complete footwork. Practice it without the ball until the tempo is natural. The first two steps are fairly slow. The third speeds up a little and the fourth step—the slide—is a little faster. Here's the rhythm:

Right . . . left . . . right . . . slide.

That rhythm is important in timing.

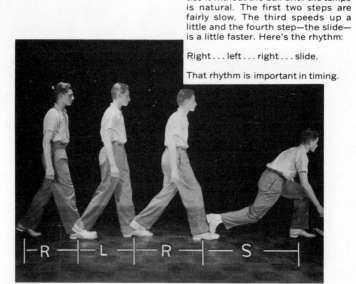

When the footwork rhythm feels natural, try it with the swing to coordinate your arm movement with your footwork. Here's your starting position—the same as in the push-and-swing delivery. Left foot slightly forward, most of your weight on the left foot, knees relaxed, body upright and relaxed, the ball in both hands with most of its weight supported by your left hand.

On your first step, ball and foot start forward together. As you step forward with your right foot, push the ball straight forward just as in the push-swing delivery. On this step your ball does not start its downward swing. Your timing should be such that as your right foot touches the floor the ball is directly over it.

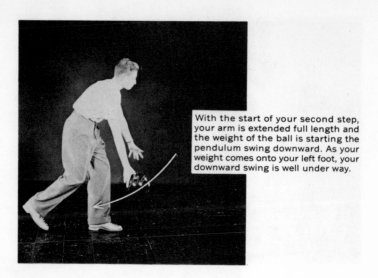

With the start of your second step, your arm is extended full length and the weight of the ball is starting the pendulum swing downward. As your weight comes onto your left foot, your downward swing is well under way.

Now the third step . . . a little faster. And here your timing should bring you into fine balance on your left foot . . . the ball and your right foot passing each other at the bottom of the pendulum arc and your body moving smoothly forward.

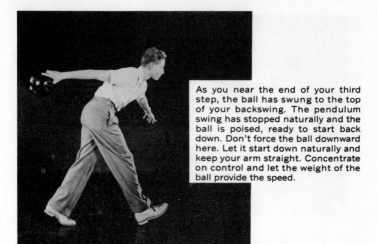

As you near the end of your third step, the ball has swung to the top of your backswing. The pendulum swing has stopped naturally and the ball is poised, ready to start back down. Don't force the ball downward here. Let it start down naturally and keep your arm straight. Concentrate on control and let the weight of the ball provide the speed.

Your swing starts down as you start your last step, which is the slide. Throughout this last step, the ball and left foot are moving forward together... then...

... as you slide forward and the straight-arm, pendulum swing brings the ball low ...

... and across the foul line, you release it smoothly just ahead of your left foot. Your right foot remains extended to the rear to maintain balance, and your right arm swings on upward in a full, smooth follow-through.

There is the whole movement for the four-step delivery—arms and feet timed in a smooth rhythm of—right... left... right... slide and swing, right ...left... right... slide and swing.

Practice this approach and swing over and over until the movement, the flow and the rhythm are as natural as dancing—until arms and feet coordinate naturally. Then...

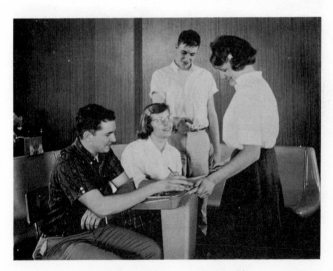

... you're well on your way to a life-time of fun, as a participant in America's favorite indoor sport.

3

AIMING

After the fundamentals, timing and rhythm of the approach and delivery have become natural to you, you will find yourself releasing the ball at exactly the same spot and in exactly the same direction every time. This is the time to begin studying the technique of aiming.

For a right-handed bowler, the best "strike ball," one that knocks down all the pins, is one that hits between the 1 pin and the 3 pin from an angle to the right of the head pin ... right into what is called the 1-3 "pocket." In modern bowling ...

SPOT BOWLING
WITH
THE RANGE FINDER SYSTEM

... the best method of putting your ball into that 1-3 pocket every time is called "spot bowling," a technique in which you use the Range Finder system to help you aim.

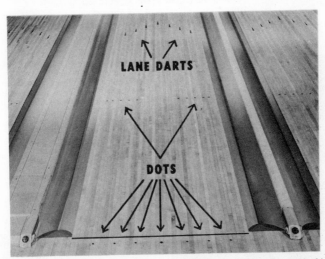

LANE DARTS

DOTS

Consisting of a series of dots and arrows called "lane darts," the Range Finder system is designed to help you "line up" your shot by giving you several aiming points instead of just one. In addition to the different marking combinations for a strike ball ...

...there are dozens of possible marking combinations for a "spare" ball ...a second ball which knocks down all the pins the first ball has missed. Finding the proper line of sight to roll the various strike and spare balls...

...is a matter of trial and error until you have determined which combination of Range Finder markings is best for each one. Your instructor will be happy to help you work them out, and once you've learned them...

...you'll find the spot system of bowling will greatly increase your aiming power. One of the most important factors in selecting the proper Range Finder markings is the kind of ball you roll. There are three kinds of balls...

STRAIGHT BALL

. . . the straight ball, the hook ball, and the back-up ball. Since all balls have some spin imparted to them naturally at the point of release . . .

. . . the straight ball is not really a "straight ball" in the true sense of the word. It does not follow a perfectly straight course, but because it does not have a great deal of spin, it usually does not definitely "break" or curve before it reaches the pins. If the straight ball is used . . .

. . . the ball should be gripped so that the palm of the hand is directly underneath, with the thumb straight up.

This grip is maintained throughout the delivery, and at the point of release...

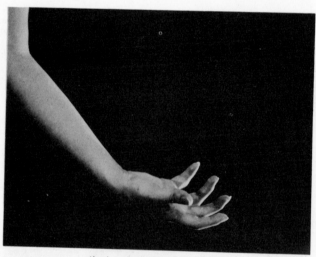

...the hand still remains in the same position, with no wrist action as the ball leaves the fingers. After the ball is released...

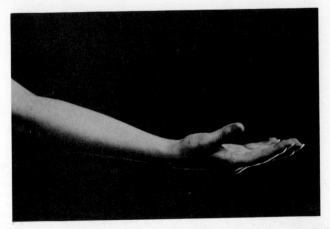

... the bowler "follows through" by letting the arm flow out naturally until the hand is brought up to eye level ... "reaching" for the pins, palm up. Wrist action is <u>not</u> used with the straight ball and the "line of sight" is a straight line from the right of the approach to the 1-3 pocket.

However, since the ball <u>will</u> spin slightly, no matter what you do, the sooner you begin making that spin work <u>for</u> you, the sooner you'll increase your scores.

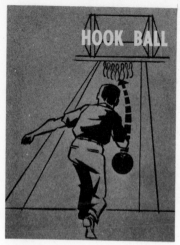

HOOK BALL

The hook ball for instance, is rolled by twisting the wrist slightly to the left. This develops a counterclockwise spin in the ball, causing it to travel toward the pins in an arc, angling across the lane into the 1·3 pocket and increasing your chances of knocking down more pins. To roll the hook ball . . .

. . . start by gripping the ball so that the palm of your hand is slightly to the right of the underside of the ball.

Hold this position during the delivery,
and as you start your release . . .

. . . the weight of the ball, plus the forward swing of your arm, will bring the
thumb out first. As soon as the thumb
is out . . .

... lift with your fingers and turn your wrist over. The lift gives direction, and the wrist turn imparts the desired spin to the ball. After the release...

... follow through by bringing the hand up to the level of the eyes, palm down, and "reaching" for the pins. Both of these balls, the hook, and when rolled naturally, even the straight ball...

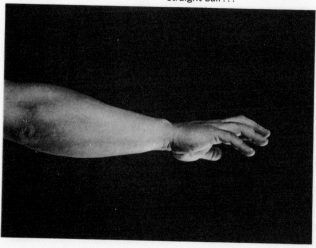

. . . have varying degrees of counter-clockwise spin. In contrast to this, the remaining ball . . .

. . . the back-up ball, spins in a clock-wise direction. The effect of this spin is exactly the same in that it causes the ball to "break" or travel in an arc on its way to the pins. Only this time . . .

BACK-UP BALL

BACK-UP BALL

... the "break" is from left to right, instead of from right to left. While this clockwise spin is necessary for left-handed bowlers who wish to hook or curve their balls ...

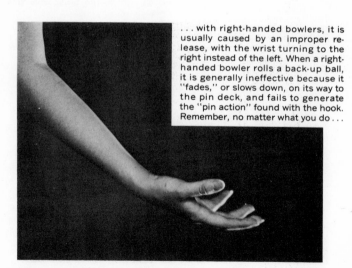

... with right-handed bowlers, it is usually caused by an improper release, with the wrist turning to the right instead of the left. When a right-handed bowler rolls a back-up ball, it is generally ineffective because it "fades," or slows down, on its way to the pin deck, and fails to generate the "pin action" found with the hook. Remember, no matter what you do ...

. . . you will impart <u>some</u> spin to the ball at the point of release. So learn to control it!

Practice your aiming and delivery until you have that spin working <u>for</u> you instead of against you, and enjoy the increased thrills and higher scores that are a natural result of a well-rolled hook.

59

4

SCORING

Every bowler should be able to score a game and while bowling's scoring system may look complicated at first, actually it becomes very simple after a little study. Here are the fundamentals.

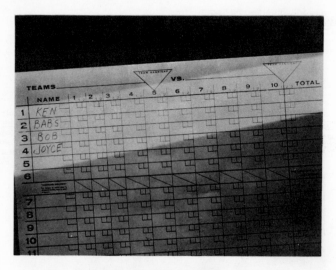

Each line on the score sheet represents a game for one player and each line is made up of ten squares, or frames. Thus, ten frames make one game.

For every frame a player may roll his ball twice. In bowling, these two balls constitute a player's "turn," and each frame on the score sheet contains two squares, one for each ball.

The number of pins knocked down by the first ball . . . in this case, 3 . . . is . marked in the first small square.

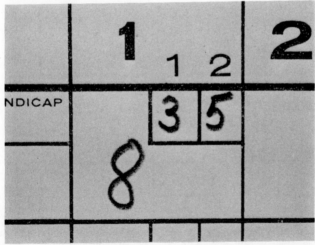

The number knocked down by the second ball . . . 5 in this example . . . is marked in the second box. Then the two figures are added . . .

. . . giving the bowler a total <u>frame</u> score of 8 for the frame.

Some score sheets have only one small square in each frame. In this case...

...the number of pins knocked down by the first ball is marked just outside the square and the number for the second ball is marked inside the square. Score is progressive with each frame. For example...

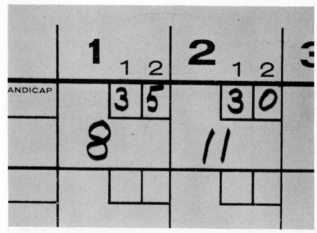

...assume you had 8 in the first frame. Then, in your second frame, you got 3 pins with your first ball and none with your second, giving you a total in that <u>frame</u> of 3. To figure your <u>game</u> score, you'd simply add the 3 you got in the second frame to the 8 you had in the first frame...

...giving you a total <u>game</u> score of 11 in the second frame. In addition to this straight progressive scoring...

... special bonuses are given for strikes and spares. Although beginning bowlers sometimes experience difficulty in scoring strikes and spares, once again, it's only a matter of learning a few simple fundamentals.

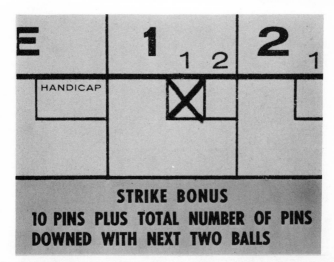

STRIKE BONUS
10 PINS PLUS TOTAL NUMBER OF PINS DOWNED WITH NEXT TWO BALLS

A strike is marked with an "X" in the first small box ...

... and the strike bonus is 10 pins, plus the total number of pins knocked down with the next two balls. For example ...

. . . let's say you rolled a strike with your very first ball. Since your strike bonus is 10, plus the total number of pins knocked down with your next two balls, you can't score the frame until you've rolled your next two balls. When your second turn comes up . . .

. . . you knock down 3 pins with the first ball and 4 with the second, for a frame total of 7. Now you're ready to score the first frame. Since your strike bonus is 10 plus the total number of pins knocked down with the next two balls, and the two balls you rolled in the second frame netted a total of 7 pins . . .

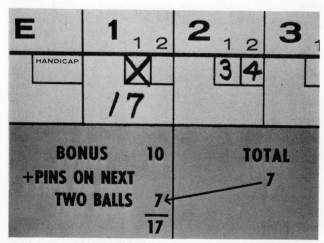

. . . simply add the 7 to the base figure of 10 and your score for the first frame is 17. Now, since the score is progressive, to figure your game score for frame 2, simply take the 17 you had in the first frame . . .

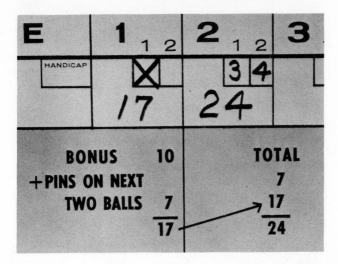

... add it to the 7 you earned in the second frame and you have your game score so far ... 24. In this case the 7 is added twice ...

... first, as part of the bonus for the strike you rolled in the first frame, and again as your total "turn" score for the second frame. The same rule applies regardless of how many strikes in a row are rolled. For instance ...

... let's assume you "got hot" and rolled two strikes in a row. Following the bonus rule, the strike you got in frame one is worth 10 plus the pins knocked down with the next <u>two</u> balls. But your strike in the second frame is only one ball, so you must wait to see what you get with your first ball in frame three before you can figure your score for frame one.

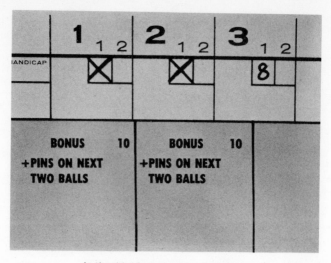

In the third frame you knocked down
8 pins with your first ball. Now you
can compute your score.

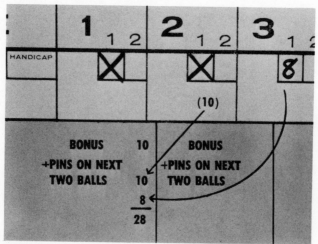

First go back to frame one. The bonus
for your first strike is 10, plus the 10
for the pins you knocked down with
your strike in frame two, plus 8 for

the pins you got with your first ball in
frame three . . . giving you a total of
28 in the first frame.

With your second ball in frame three, you knocked down 1 pin, and now you can figure your score for the second frame.

The bonus for your strike in the second frame is 10, plus the 8 for the pins you knocked down with your first ball in frame three, plus 1 for the pin you knocked down with your second ball . . . giving you a frame score of 19. To figure your <u>game</u> score, add to the 19, the 28 you earned in the first frame, and you see that your game score is 47. Continuing to frame three . . .

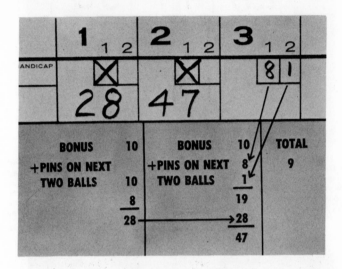

. . . you had a total for that <u>frame</u> of 9. Add to this the "47" that represented your <u>game</u> score in frame two and in the <u>third</u> frame you have a game score of 56. In this case . . .

1 1 2	2 1 2	3 1 2
HANDICAP ☒	☒	8 1
28	47	56

BONUS	10	BONUS	10	TOTAL
+PINS ON NEXT		+PINS ON NEXT	8	8
TWO BALLS	10	TWO BALLS	1	1
	8		19	47
	28		28	56
			47	

... the 8 you got with your first ball in the third frame was added three times ... once as part of the bonus for your first strike, again as part of the bonus for your second strike, and still again, as part of your frame total for frame three.

The one pin you got with your second ball in the third frame was added twice ... once as part of the bonus for your second strike, and again as part of your frame total for frame three. For instance, if your first ball left three pins standing ...

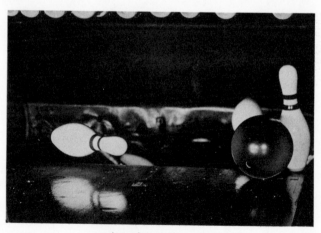

... and you knock them down with your second ball, you have "picked up" your spare and are entitled to a "spare bonus."

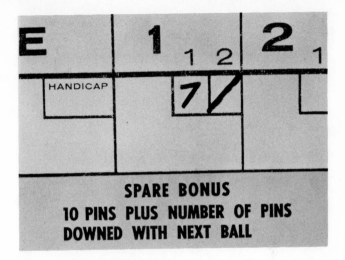

SPARE BONUS
10 PINS PLUS NUMBER OF PINS DOWNED WITH NEXT BALL

A spare is marked with a single diagonal stroke in the second small square . . .

. . . and the spare bonus is, 10 pins, plus the number of pins knocked down with the next ball. To see how this works . . .

. . . let's say you knocked down 4 pins with your first ball and 6 with your second, giving you a spare for the first frame. Since the spare bonus is 10 plus the number of pins knocked down with the next ball, you must wait until you've rolled your next ball before you can figure your score.

Your first ball in frame two gets 6 pins. Add the 6 to the spare bonus of 10 and your game score in the first frame is 16. Now you roll your second ball . . .

. . . and get two more pins for a frame total of 8 in the second frame. To determine your game score . . .

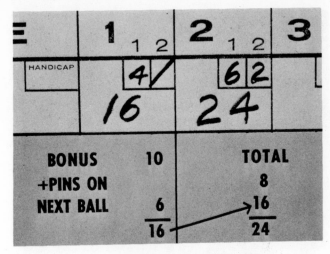

	1			2			3
		1	2		1	2	
HANDICAP		4	/		6	2	
	16			24			

BONUS	10	TOTAL
+PINS ON		8
NEXT BALL	6	16
	16	24

. . . simply add to the frame total of 8, the 16 you had for the first frame, and your game score in the second frame is 24. The spare bonus is figured the same way as the strike bonus, regardless of how many spares in a row you roll.

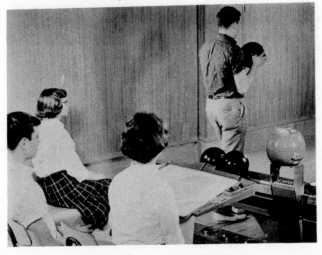

To understand this scoring system more clearly let's watch how Ken's game is scored here.

On his first frame his second ball
leaves two pins standing.

His score sheet records each ball. Five
on the first one—three on the second
—a total score of eight for the first
frame.

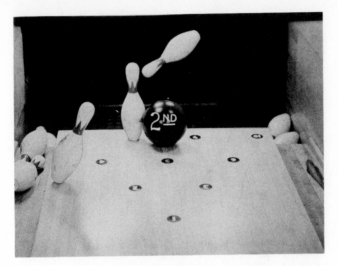

On Ken's second frame he gets a spare—his second ball takes out all the remaining pins.

The score sheet records the spare in the second small square with a diagonal line. But we cannot total the score yet. He still has his spare bonus from the first ball in his next frame.

On his next turn to bowl, Ken's first ball takes six pins.

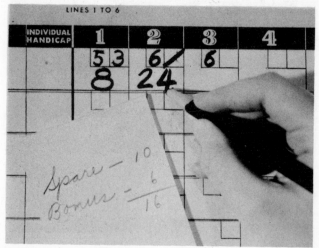

Now, we can total the score for frame two. Ten points for the spare plus six for his bonus is sixteen. We add sixteen to the score for the first frame. His score totals twenty-four in the second frame, and he has one more ball in his third frame, with four pins still standing.

And he gets them. All the pins down
in two balls, so he has another spare.

We can mark his spare but we can't
compute his score for the frame yet,
because he still has his bonus for the
spare—the score of the first ball in
his next frame.

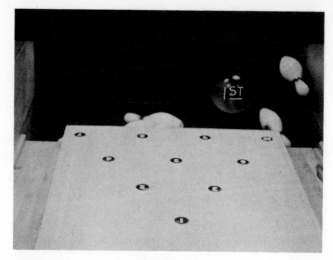

Now, Ken is really warming up. The first ball in frame four takes out all the pins—a strike.

We mark the strike in frame four and now, we can figure his score for frame three. Ten for the spare plus ten for his score on the first ball in the next frame—that's twenty. Add twenty to the score in the second frame, and Ken has a score of forty-four in his third frame.

In frame five, Ken runs into tough luck...after two balls, he leaves three pins still standing. He knocked down seven pins, so...

...seven in his bonus for his strike in frame four—one on the first ball and six on the second. Ten for the strike...seven for the bonus... makes seventeen for the frame...a total score of sixty-one in his fourth frame.

Then add his score of seven in the fifth frame, and he has a total of sixty-eight in his fifth frame.

In the sixth frame, Ken gets another strike.

All we can do now is mark it as a strike and wait to see what his bonus will be from his next two balls.

Frame seven, another strike. Now, he's really bowling.

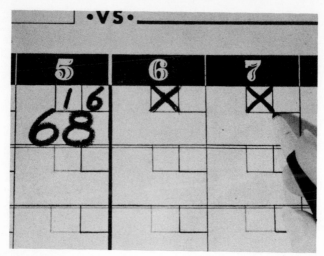

We can mark his strike for frame seven but we still cannot compute his score for frame six, because his strike bonus, remember, is the total score of his next two balls, and he only used one ball on frame seven. We'll have to wait for his next ball to complete frame six.

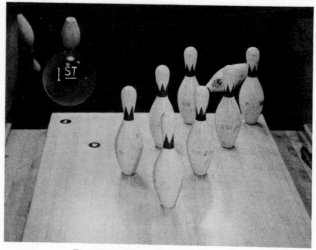

The first ball in the eighth frame knocks down three pins.

Now we can compute his score for frame six. He gets ten for his strike in frame six ... plus ten and three for the scores of his next two balls. Twenty-three for frame six, for a total score of ninety-one in the sixth frame.

Ken's second ball in frame eight gets only three more pins.

Now we can bring his score up to date. In frame seven, he gets the total of his two balls in frame eight as a bonus. Ten for the strike and six for the bonus is sixteen. Sixteen plus his previous score of ninety-one gives him a hundred and seven in frame seven.

Then add his six points for the two balls in frame eight and he has a hundred and thirteen points with two frames to go. That's not bad bowling.

82

In frame nine he ran into tough luck again. Eight on his first ball and none on his second. Now his total score is one hundred and twenty-one.

But on his tenth and last frame, Ken is back in form again—another strike.

We can mark his strike, but he still has his bonus coming. On the tenth frame, you don't wait for your next turn to take your bonus rolls. If you have a strike, you roll two extra balls immediately. If you have a spare, you roll one extra ball immediately.

Ken's still in form. Both his bonus balls get strikes.

Now we can finish his score. Ten for the strike in the tenth frame . . . ten for the first bonus ball and ten for the second—a total of thirty points for the tenth frame and that completes the game . . .

. . . with a total score of 151. That's not bad at all. To keep score quickly and easily, just remember the two bonus "rules" . . .

85

STRIKE BONUS
10 PINS PLUS TOTAL NUMBER OF PINS
DOWNED WITH NEXT TWO BALLS

... the strike bonus being 10 pins
plus the total number of pins knocked
down with the next two balls ...

SPARE BONUS
10 PINS PLUS NUMBER OF PINS
DOWNED WITH NEXT BALL

... and the spare bonus being 10
pins plus the number of pins knocked
down with the next ball. If you'll learn
these two rules, you'll find scoring is
simply a matter of paying attention to
each roll.

Whether your score is high or low, whether you're winner or loser, there's a lifetime of fun in bowling. The real satisfaction is in good health from good exercise, the friendly competition and the recreation that makes for fuller living.

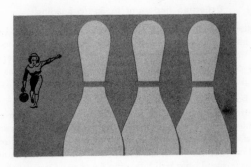

MAKING THOSE SPARES

"Make the spares and the strikes will take care of themselves."

This old expression stresses a fundamental necessity for bowling a good game. Strikes are wonderful to get, and look nice on the score sheet, but, for the average bowler, it's the spares that really count. Unless the bowler can convert leaves into spares, he will seldom bowl over 120 or 130, even though he may get 3 or 4 or as many as 5 strikes per game. The bowler who makes most of his spares is virtually assured of bowling 150 or better.

Spare bowling, to be successful, requires a little thought. The bowler must know the relative positions of the various pins. When he leaves pins standing after his first ball, he must analyze them, and figure out exactly what he must do to knock all of them down. After a while, the bowler should get to recognize all of the common leaves instantly, and know exactly how they must be made.

In attempting to convert spares in which there are several pins standing, the bowler should realize that his ball does not have to strike ALL the pins—that pins which the ball could never touch CAN be knocked down by pins which the ball can touch. Hence, the bowler must not only consider how to hit the pins, but also how to hit the pins so that the pins he hits will knock down other pins.

Deflection Important In Spare Bowling

Another important thing to remember is deflection. Unless a ball hits a pin fully, the ball will be deflected from its course every time it hits a pin. The amount of deflection depends mainly on the speed of the ball, the weight of the pins, and the angle at which the ball hits the pins.

The bowler who knows about deflection can put it to good use many, many times, for a ball that is deflected can cover a greater area and hence pick up more pins. Conversely, there are times whn deflection is harmful (as in a tandem leave) and the bowler must try to avoid it. The three things to remember are (1) if a ball hits a pin head on, it is not deflected, (2) if a ball hits a pin on the right side, the ball is deflected to the right, and (3) if a ball hits a pin on the pin's left side, the ball will be deflected to the left.

How Fast To Bowl?

Speed is also important in spare bowling. Pins hit by a ball that is moving very fast will not have time to fall into a horizontal position as they move backward. Hence, there is less chance for them to knock down other pins. Pins hit by a slow ball will usually have time to fall into a horizontal position, increasing the possibility of their knocking down pins to the rear. This does not mean that a bowler should roll a slow ball in every spare attempt, but there are times when a slow ball increases the bowler's chances of making the spare. Remember, too, that a slow ball will be deflected more than a fast ball.

Here's another tip! Pins in the last row are about three feet behind the head pin, so the ball must travel further to reach them than it does to reach other pins. The bowler who rolls a hook should especially remember this fact, particularly if his ball consistantly misses pins on the same side.

Where To Roll The Ball

At which side of the lane should the bowler start his delivery for spare attempts? While there is no hard and fast rule on this matter, there is a general rule which will help considerably.

If the pin or pins are on the right side of the lane, the bowler should start left of the spot where he ordinarily rolls. How far left he should move depends on the position of the pins, and the type of ball he rolls. Hook bowlers should move further left than straight-ball rollers.

If the pin or pins are on the left side of the lane, the bowler should roll his ball from the right side, at about the same place where he rolls his strike ball. A pin or pins in the center of the lane should be aimed at from the right side of the lane, as this is the most natural and comfortable position. For left-handed bowlers, the rule is merely reversed.

The following series of drawings shows many of the common leaves which a bowler can expect to see, and explains the best way for a bowler to make them. There are, of course, other types of spares, but they are usually similar to the ones shown here, and can be converted by applying the same bowling principles.

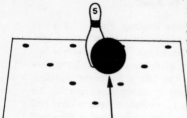

5-PIN SPARE
To convert the 5-pin spare, the ball should be rolled from the right side of the lane, and should be aimed to hit the pin squarely. Do not roll the ball down the center of the lane.

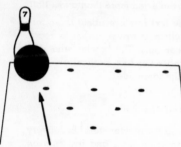

7-PIN SPARE
Start your ball at the far right side of the lane, aiming it to angle completely across the lane into the 7 pin. Remember that your ball has to travel further to make this spare.

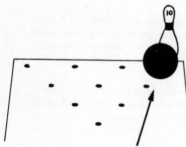

10-PIN SPARE
The 10 pin is best converted by rolling the ball from the center of the lane, or a little left of center. If your ball hooks, move left even more. Aim to hit the pin fully, or on the left side.

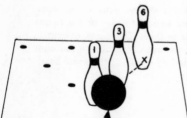

1-3-6 SPARE
Bowl the ball from the left side of the lane so that it hits between the 1 and 3 pins. Then either the ball or the 3 pin will carry the 6 pin. This leave can also be made by hitting the 1 pin on the left side so that it bounces squarely into the 3 and 6 pins, but this is not a safe method.

2-4-7 SPARE

Start the ball from the right side of the lane, and aim to hit between the 2 and 4 pins. Then, the ball or the 4 pin will bounce into the 7 pin. This can also be made by hitting the 2 pin on the right side so that it goes squarely into the 4 and 7 pins, but this is not recommended.

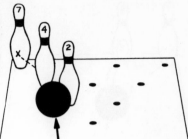

3-6-10 SPARE

Starting the ball from about the center of the lane, angle it across to hit between the 3 and 6 pins. Either the ball or the 6 pin will then carry the 10 pin. As in the previous two examples, the ball must not hit the lead pin head on, but at an angle, so that it is deflected in toward the remaining pins.

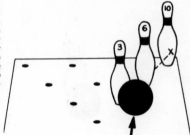

2-7 SPLIT

To convert this baby split, the ball should be rolled from the center-right side of the lane. It should glance off of the left side of the 2 pin and into the 7 pin. This split can also be made by hitting the 2 pin on the right side so that the 2 pin is hit directly into the 7 pin, but this is a risky method.

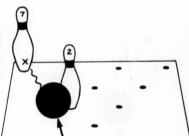

3-10 SPLIT

This split is best made by rolling the ball from the left side of the lane so that it glances off the right side of the 3 pin into the 10 pin. It can be converted by hitting the 3 pin on the left side and bouncing it into the 10 pin, but such a method is uncertain. By fitting the ball between the pins, the bowler is at least assured of getting the 10 pin should the 3 pin be missed narrowly.

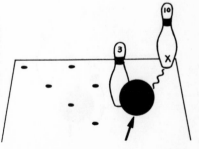

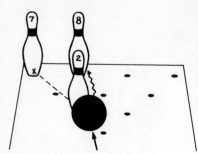

2-7-8 SPLIT

A difficult spare! It is best made by hitting the 2 pin fairly full on the right side so that it bounces into the 7 pin. The ball then carries the 8 pin. If the ball hits the 2 pin a little more fully, the 2 pin will often carry both the 7 and 8 pins, especially if the ball is moving fairly slow. The ball should be rolled from the right side of the center of the lane.

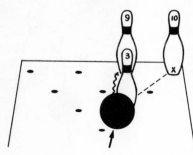

3-9-10 SPLIT

This leave is similar to the 2-7-8 split (above). The ball should be rolled from the left-center of the lane to hit on the left side of the 3 pin. The 3 pin carries the 10 pin; the ball carries the 9 pin. Or, the 3 pin carries both the other pins. In some cases, this split can be made by hitting the 3 pin full on the right side, so that the ball deflects slightly to fit between the 9 and 10 pins.

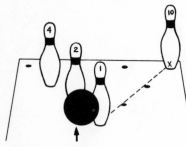

1-2-4-10 SPARE

The ball should be aimed from near the center of the lane to hit the head pin half-full. The head pin slides across the pin deck to hit the 10 pin, while the ball is deflected to carry the 2 and 4 pins.

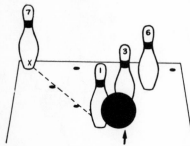

1-3-6-7 SPARE

Roll the ball from the right side of the lane. The ball should hit the 1-3 pocket like a good strike hit. This will cause the 1 pin to be knocked into the 7 pin while the ball sweeps into the 3 and 6 pins. Concentrate on hitting the 1 pin into the 7 pin; the other two pins will then be taken care of.

1-2-4-7 SPARE

To convert this spare, the ball should be rolled from the right side of the lane so that it hits the head pin on the left side. The ball will then be deflected into the rest of the setup, knocking out the 2 pin, and hitting the 4 pin into the 7 pin. This spare can also be made by hitting the head pin on the right side so that it knocks the rest of the pins down in a line, but this is at best risky.

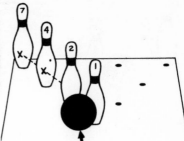

4-5 SPLIT

Great accuracy is necessary to fit the ball between the 4 and 5 pins, since the ball is only 1⅓ inches larger than the space between pins. The ball should be started from the right-center of the lane. Very infrequently, a "wild" ball will nick the outside of one pin, causing it to topple into the other, but this split should never be attempted in that manner.

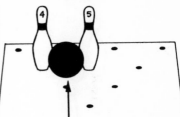

5-8-10 SPLIT

To convert this split, the ball should be bowled from the right-center or the center of the lane. It should just nick the left side of the 5 pin so that the 5 pin slides into the 10 pin. The ball carries the 8 pin.

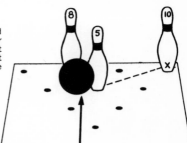

5-7-9 SPLIT

Like the previous split, the 5-7-9 is converted by sliding the 5 pin across the pin deck. The ball should be rolled from the right side of the lane so that it just nicks the 5 pin, sliding it into the 7 pin. The ball then carries the 9 pin.

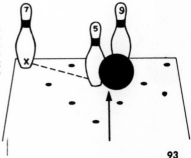

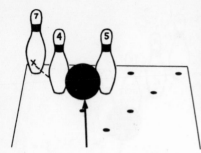

4-5-7 SPLIT
Bowl the ball from the right side of the lane. The ball should fit between the 4 and 5 pins, barely hitting the 5 pin, and hitting the 4 pin as full as possible so that it either bounces back to the 7 pin, or rebounds from the kickback into the 7 pin. This split can also be converted by barely hitting the 4 pin on the left side so that it topples into the 5 pin, the ball taking out the 7 pin, but this is a very hard shot to make.

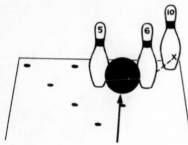

5-6-10 SPLIT
Like the 4-5-7 split, this split is best made by hitting the 5 pin thin on the right side, with the ball knocking the 6 pin off the kickback into the 10 pin. Or, a very thin hit on the right side of the 6 pin will nudge that pin into the 5, but again, this is extremely difficult, and not recommended. The ball should be rolled from the center or the left side of the lane.

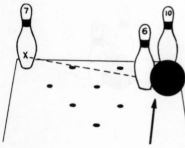

6-7-10 SPLIT
This is a fairly common split, resulting from a nose hit on the first ball. This split must be made by hitting the 6 pin very lightly on the right side so that it is sliced across the pin deck into the 7 pin. The ball carries the 10 pin. To obtain the best hitting angle for the 6 pin, the bowler should roll his ball from the center or the right side of the lane.

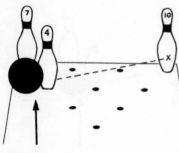

4-7-10 SPLIT
The key pin in this split is the 4 pin. It must be hit very thin on the left side so that it is sliced across the pin deck to carry the 10 pin. The ball knocks out the 7 pin. To convert this leave, the ball should be rolled from the center or the left-center of the lane.

2-4-5-8 SPARE

This spare is rather difficult, because of the 2-8 tandem. It is best made by rolling the ball from the right side of the lane, aiming it to hit rather full on the 2 pin. The 2 pin must be hit into the 4 and 8 pins, while the ball then carries the 5 pin, although it may also be deflected enough to take out the 8 pin too.

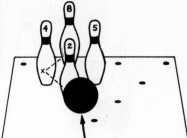

3-5-6-9 SPARE

This "right-hand bucket" is a bit more difficult than the "left-hand bucket" (above) because the ball must be rolled at a more unfavorable angle. Started from the center or the right side of the lane, the ball must hit full on the left side of the 3 pin. The 3 pin carries the 6 and 9 pins, while the ball knocks out the 5 pin, and perhaps may deflect into the 9 pin.

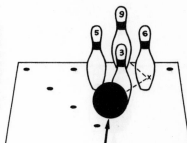

5-10 SPLIT

To convert this split, roll the ball from the center or right-center of the lane. The ball must hit the 5 pin thin on the left side, so that the 5 pin slides into the 10 pin. Don't hit the 5 pin too thin, or it will slide in front of the 10 pin.

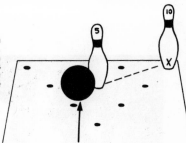

5-7 SPLIT

A ball delivered from the right side will give the best angle for hitting the 5 pin thin on the right side, deflecting it into the 7 pin. Because of the favorable angle, this split is generally easier to convert than its opposite number, the 5-10.

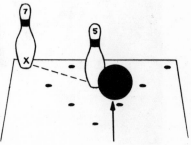

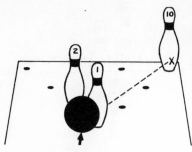

1-2-10 SPLIT

This leave is not as difficult to convert as it looks. The ball, rolled from the center of the lane, should hit the head pin medium on the left side, bouncing that pin directly into the 10 pin or off the kickback into the 10 pin. The ball rolls through to take out the 2 pin.

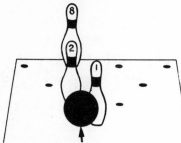

1-2-8 SPARE

This leave can be converted several ways, but the best method is to aim the ball from the right side of the lane so that it hits the head pin fairly full. The ball is then deflected slightly to hit the 2 pin on the nose, the 2 pin or the ball, then go straight back to take out the 8 pin.